Contents

About *Vocabulary Centers, Grades K–1* 2

Making a File Folder Center 3

Center Checklist 4

Color Names 5

Do They Rhyme? 23

Words to Know 39

In My Suitcase 55

School Fun 75

Make a Word 89

Two Words in One 103

"Ow" Words 117

Opposites 131

First in Line 145

Animal Babies 161

Let's Play! 177

About
Vocabulary Centers
Grades K-1

What's Great About This Book

Centers are a wonderful, fun way for students to practice important skills. The 12 centers in this book are self-contained and portable. Students may work at a desk, at a table, or even on the floor. Once you've made the centers, they're ready to use any time.

What's in This Book

Teacher and student directions include how to make and use the center

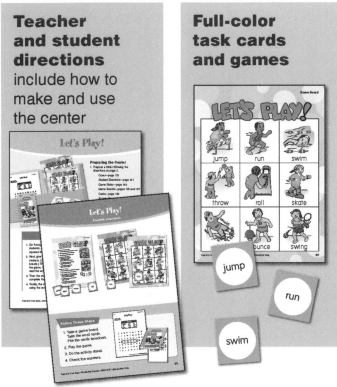

Full-color task cards and games

Reproducible activity sheets to practice vocabulary skills

Self-checking answer keys

How to Use the Centers

The centers are intended for skill practice, not to introduce skills. It is important to model the use of each center before students do the task independently.

Questions to Consider:

- Will students select a center, or will you assign the centers?
- Will there be a specific block of time for centers, or will the centers be used throughout the day?
- Where will you place the centers for easy access by students?
- What procedure will students use when they need help with the center tasks?
- How will you track the tasks and centers completed by each student?

Making a File Folder Center

Materials:

- folder with pockets
- envelopes
- marking pens and pencils
- scissors
- stapler
- glue or two-sided tape
- paper fasteners
- small objects for markers (e.g., dried beans, pennies, etc.)

Folder Back

Folder Front

Steps to Follow:

1. Laminate the cover. Tape it to the front of the folder.

2. Laminate the student directions page. Tape it to the back of the folder.

3. Laminate the self-checking answer key for each center. Cut the page in half. Staple the cover on top of the answer key. Place the answer key in the left-hand pocket.

4. Place activity sheets and any other supplies in the left-hand pocket.

5. Laminate the task cards and puzzle pieces. Place each set in a labeled envelope in the right-hand pocket.

6. If needed for a center, laminate the sorting mat or game board and place it in the right-hand pocket of the folder.

Center Checklist

Student Names

Centers

Color Names											
Do They Rhyme?											
Words to Know											
In My Suitcase											
School Fun											
Make a Word											
Two Words in One											
"Ow" Words											
Opposites											
First in Line											
Animal Babies											
Let's Play!											

Color Names

Preparing the Center

1. Prepare a folder following the directions on page 3.

    Cover—page 7

    Student Directions—page 9

    Game Rules—page 11

    Game Board—pages 13 and 15

    Spinner Pieces—page 17

    Game Pieces—page 19

    Answer Key—page 21

2. Reproduce a supply of the activity sheet on page 6. Place copies in the left-hand pocket of the folder.

Small-Group Practice

1. Each student takes a bunny playing piece and places it on the Start square on the game board. Go through the game rules and demonstrate how to use the spinner and move the playing pieces.

2. The students take turns spinning and moving their playing pieces on the board. They continue to play until one player reaches the Winner square.

3. Then the students work cooperatively to complete their own activity sheet.

4. Finally, the students check their answers using the answer key.

Independent Practice

1. The student takes the game board, the spinner, and a playing piece. Go through the game rules and show the student how to play the game.

2. Next, the student places the bunny playing piece on the Start square on the game board. The student spins and moves the playing piece until he or she reaches the Winner square.

3. Then the student completes the activity sheet.

4. Finally, the student self-checks by using the answer key.

Color Names

Color some parts. Use the box. Then color the rest.

Colors			
1. blue	2. green	3. brown	4. red
5. yellow	6. orange	7. purple	8. tan

Color Names

Student Directions

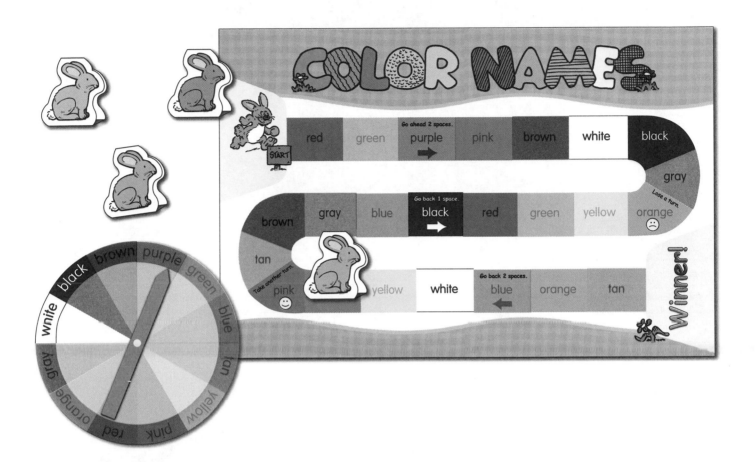

Follow These Steps

1. Take the spinner, a bunny, and the game board.

2. Play the game.

3. Do the activity sheet.

4. Check your answers.

COLOR NAMES

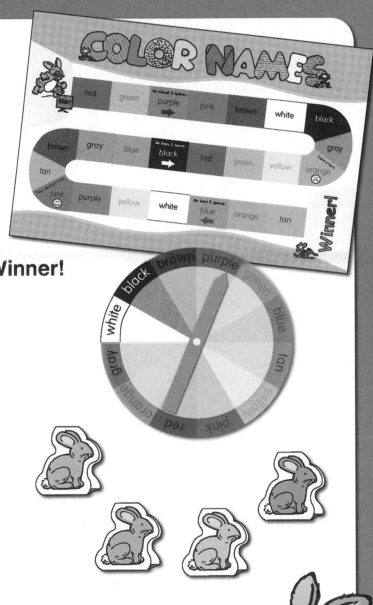

Rules for a Small Group:

1. Pick a bunny. Put it on **Start**.

2. Spin the spinner.

3. Read the color word.

4. Move your bunny to that color.

5. Take turns playing the game. Play until one bunny reaches **Winner!**

Rules for 1 Player:

1. Pick a bunny. Put it on **Start**.

2. Spin the spinner.

3. Read the color word.

4. Move your bunny to that color.

5. Play until you reach **Winner!**

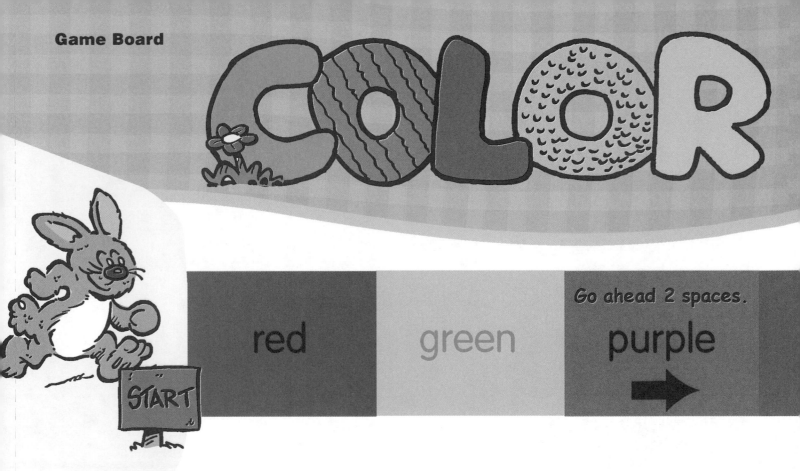

COLOR

red

green

Go ahead 2 spaces.
purple →

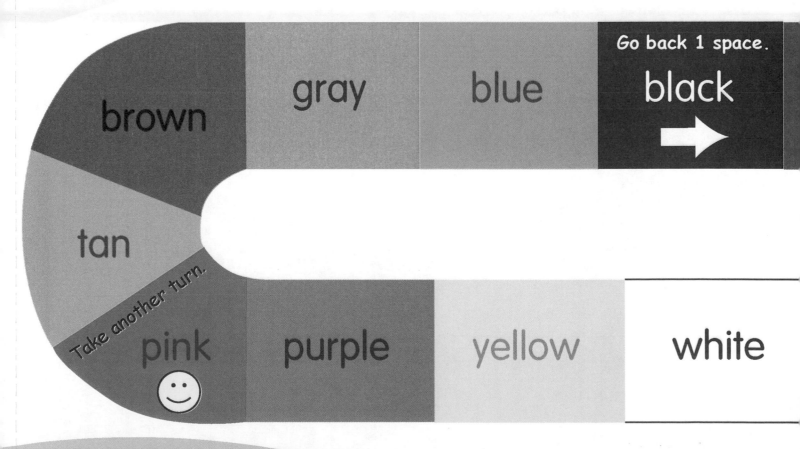

brown

gray

blue

Go back 1 space.
black →

tan

Take another turn.

pink ☺

purple

yellow

white

| pink | brown | white | black |

gray

Lose a turn.

| red | green | yellow | orange |

😞

Go back 2 spaces.

| blue | orange | tan |

←

Winner!

Use a paper fastener to attach the arrow to the spinner.

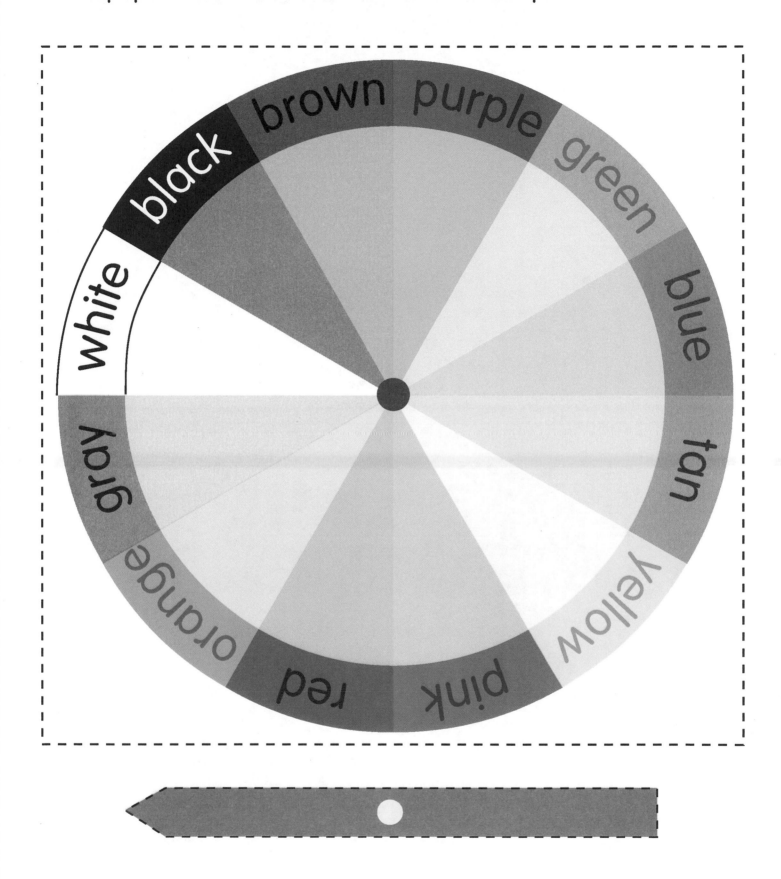

Color Names

EMC 3347 • © Evan-Moor Corp.

Color Names

EMC 3347 • © Evan-Moor Corp.

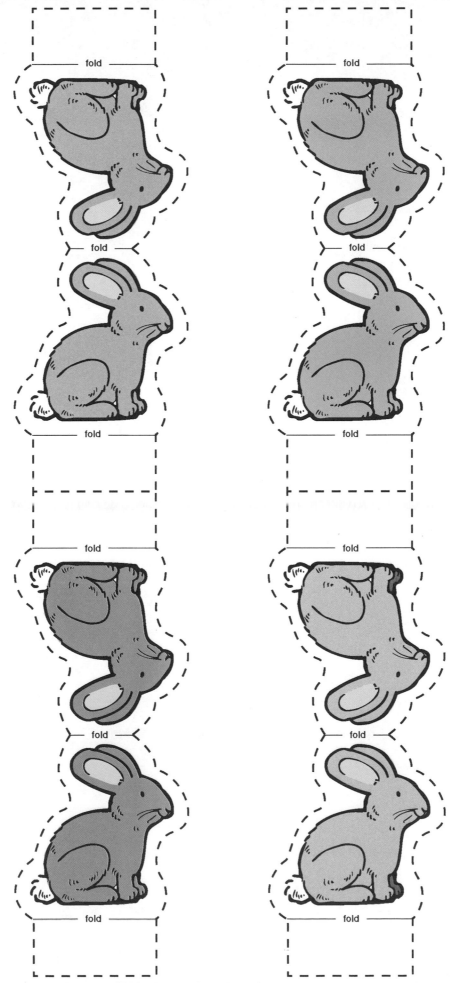

Color Names

Lift the flap to check your answers.

Do They Rhyme?

Preparing the Center

1. Prepare a folder following the directions on page 3.

   Cover—page 25

   Student Directions—page 27

   Puzzle Pieces—pages 29–35

   Answer Key—page 37

2. Reproduce a supply of the activity sheet on page 24. Place copies in the left-hand pocket of the folder.

Small-Group Practice

1. The students spread out the puzzle pieces faceup.

2. Next, the students take turns fitting together two words that rhyme. The students then connect the corresponding sentence piece to the two rhyming words. The students read the sentence aloud. The puzzles are self-checking.

3. Then the students work cooperatively to complete their own activity sheet.

4. Finally, the students check their answers using the answer key.

Independent Practice

1. The student spreads out the puzzle pieces faceup.

2. Next, the student fits together two words that rhyme. The student then connects the corresponding sentence piece to the two rhyming words. The student reads the sentence aloud. The puzzles are self-checking.

3. Then the student completes the activity sheet.

4. Finally, the student self-checks by using the answer key.

Do They Rhyme?

Color the shapes **brown** if the words rhyme.
Color the shapes **green** if the words do <u>not</u> rhyme.

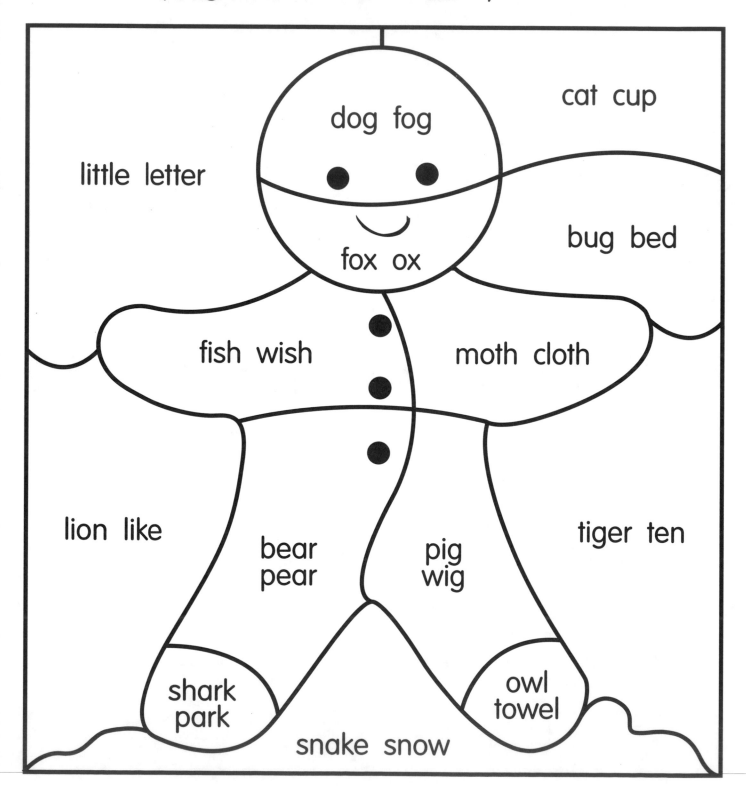

cat cup

dog fog

little letter

bug bed

fox ox

fish wish

moth cloth

lion like

bear pear

pig wig

tiger ten

shark park

owl towel

snake snow

DO THEY RHYME?

Do They Rhyme?

Follow These Steps

1. Spread out the puzzle pieces.

2. Put together two words that rhyme.

3. Fit the sentence to the rhyming words. Read the sentence out loud.

4. Make all of the puzzles.

5. Do the activity sheet.

6. Check your answers.

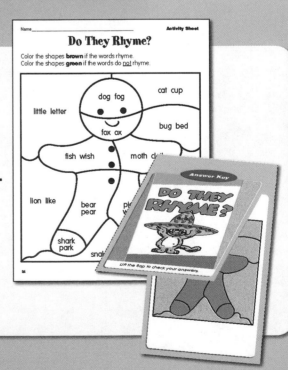

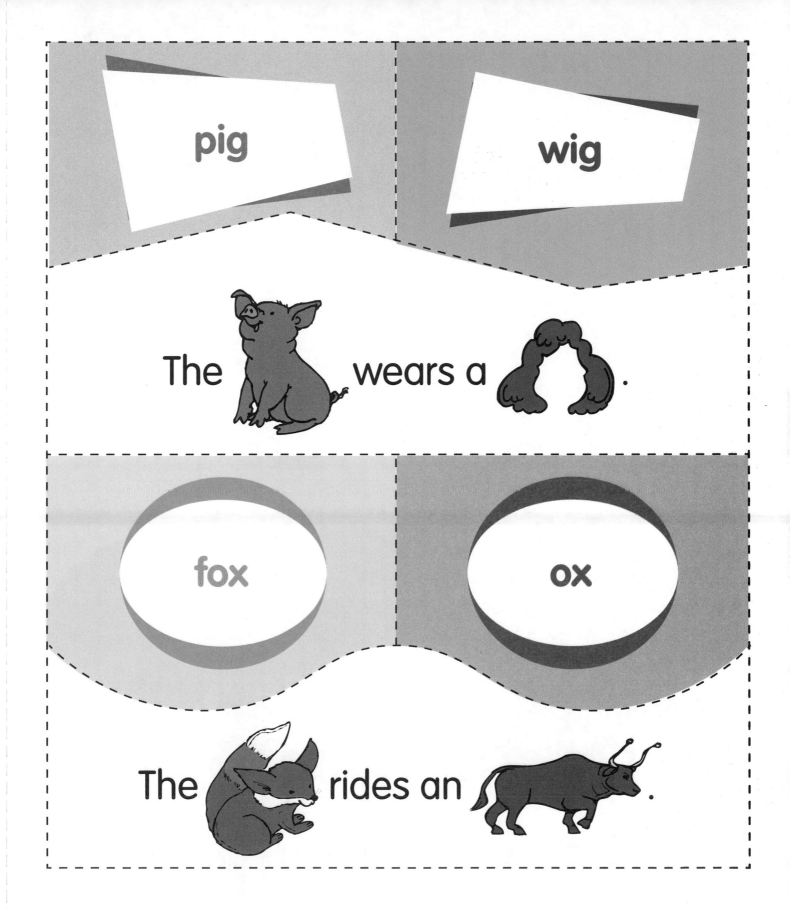

pig

wig

The 🐷 wears a 〰️.

fox

ox

The 🦊 rides an 🐂.

Do They Rhyme?
EMC 3347 • © Evan-Moor Corp.

Do They Rhyme?
EMC 3347 • © Evan-Moor Corp.

Do They Rhyme?
EMC 3347 • © Evan-Moor Corp.

Do They Rhyme?
EMC 3347 • © Evan-Moor Corp.

Do They Rhyme?
EMC 3347 • © Evan-Moor Corp.

Do They Rhyme?
EMC 3347 • © Evan-Moor Corp.

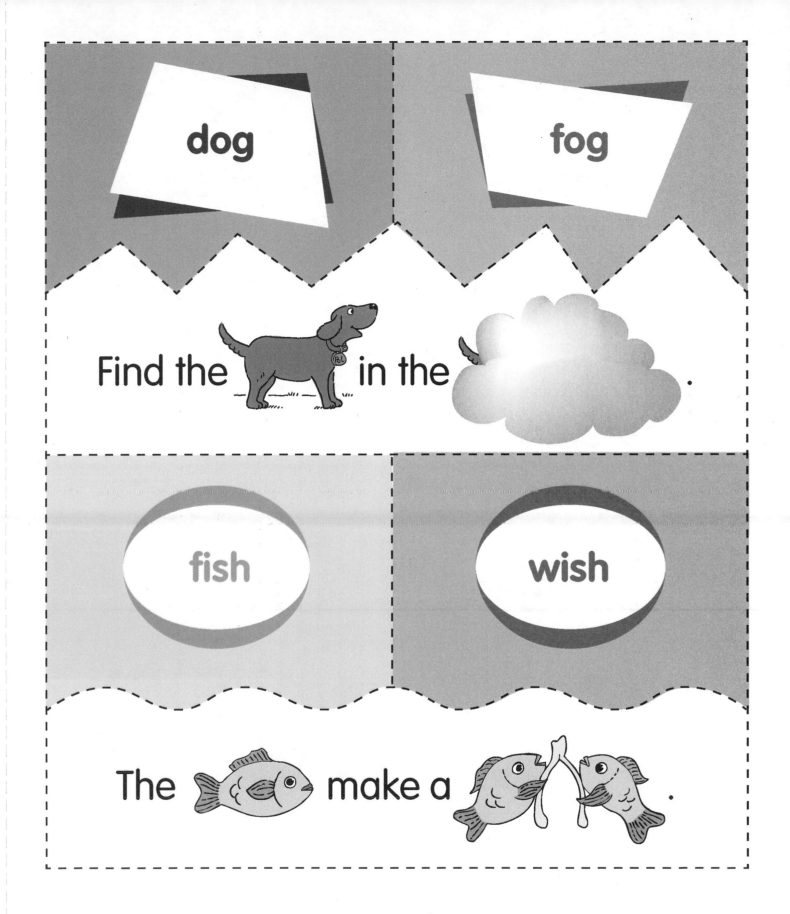

dog

fog

Find the 🐕 in the ☁.

fish

wish

The 🐟 make a 🐟🐟.

Do They Rhyme?
EMC 3347 • © Evan-Moor Corp.

Do They Rhyme?
EMC 3347 • © Evan-Moor Corp.

Do They Rhyme?
EMC 3347 • © Evan-Moor Corp.

Do They Rhyme?
EMC 3347 • © Evan-Moor Corp.

Do They Rhyme?
EMC 3347 • © Evan-Moor Corp.

Do They Rhyme?
EMC 3347 • © Evan-Moor Corp.

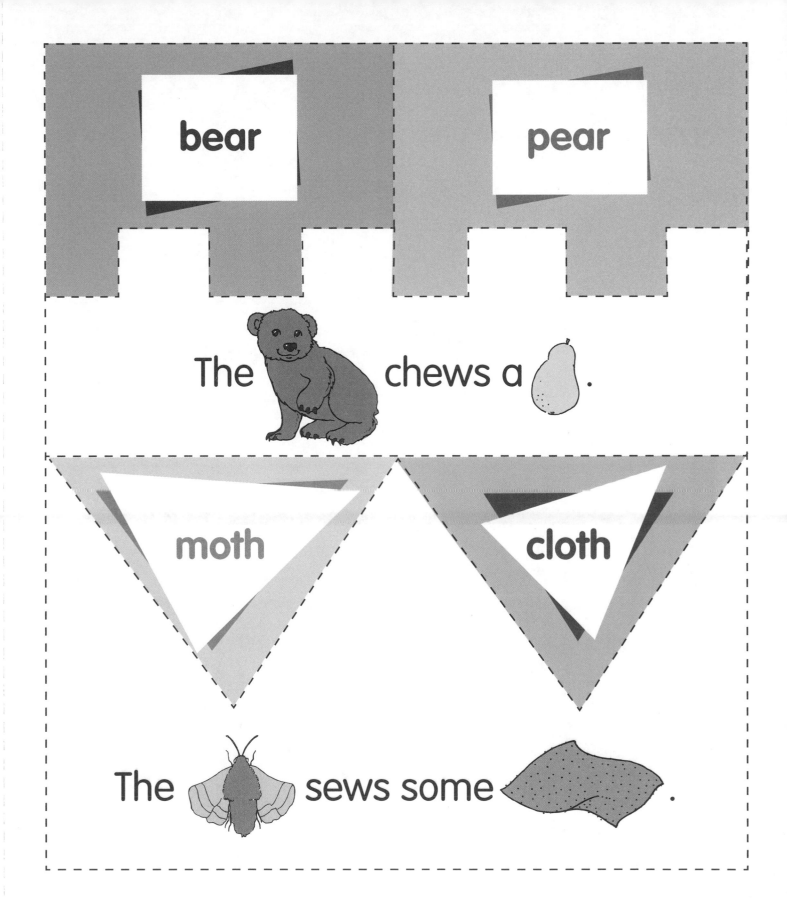

bear

pear

The [bear] chews a [pear].

moth

cloth

The [moth] sews some [cloth].

Do They Rhyme?
EMC 3347 • © Evan-Moor Corp.

Do They Rhyme?
EMC 3347 • © Evan-Moor Corp.

Do They Rhyme?
EMC 3347 • © Evan-Moor Corp.

Do They Rhyme?
EMC 3347 • © Evan-Moor Corp.

Do They Rhyme?
EMC 3347 • © Evan-Moor Corp.

Do They Rhyme?
EMC 3347 • © Evan-Moor Corp.

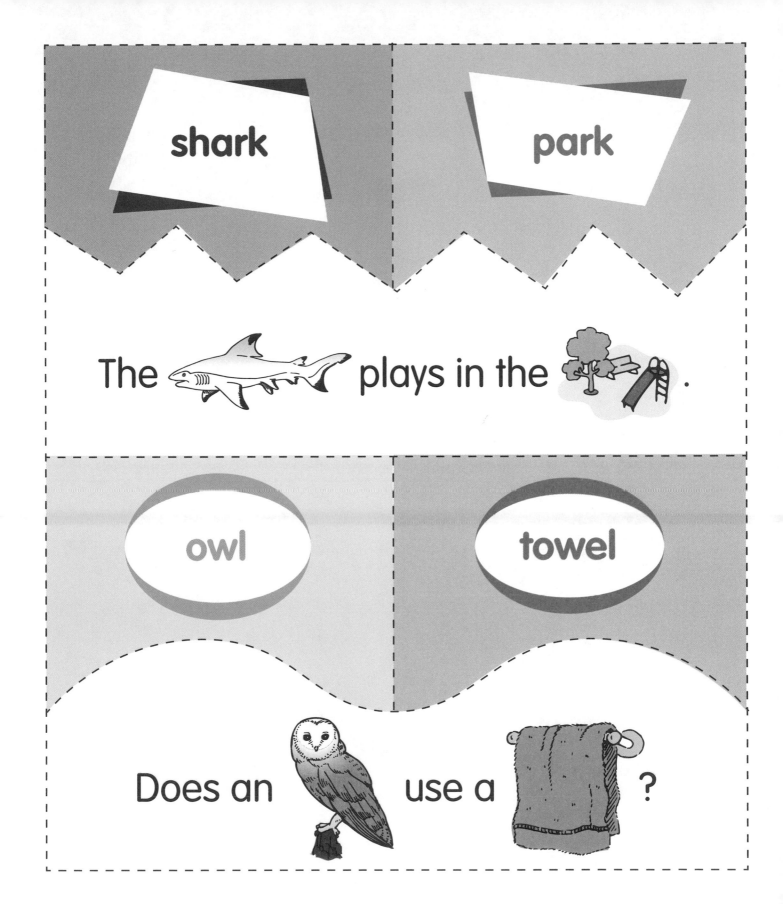

shark

park

The ~~shark~~ plays in the ~~park~~ .

owl

towel

Does an ~~owl~~ use a ~~towel~~ ?

Do They Rhyme?
EMC 3347 • © Evan-Moor Corp.

Do They Rhyme?
EMC 3347 • © Evan-Moor Corp.

Do They Rhyme?
EMC 3347 • © Evan-Moor Corp.

Do They Rhyme?
EMC 3347 • © Evan-Moor Corp.

Do They Rhyme?
EMC 3347 • © Evan-Moor Corp.

Do They Rhyme?
EMC 3347 • © Evan-Moor Corp.

Do They Rhyme?

Lift the flap to check your answers.

Words to Know

Preparing the Center

1. Prepare a folder following the directions on page 3.

    Cover—page 41

    Student Directions—page 43

    Game Rules—page 45

    Word Cards—pages 47–51

    Answer Key—page 53

2. Reproduce a supply of the activity sheet on page 40. Place copies in the left-hand pocket of the folder.

Small-Group Practice

1. Review the game rules with the students. Have the students practice reading the word cards before beginning the game. The words are sight words.

2. Next, the students play the game, trying to make the most matches.

3. Then the students work cooperatively to complete their own activity sheet.

4. Finally, the students check their answers using the answer key.

Independent Practice

1. Review the game rules with the student. Have the student practice reading the word cards before beginning the game. The words are sight words.

2. Next, the student attempts to match all the sets of cards as quickly as possible.

3. Then the student completes the activity sheet.

4. Finally, the student self-checks by using the answer key.

Words to Know

Find the words in the puzzle.
Circle them.

d o s a i d x (a r e)
h a v e p m u s t r
q w e n t b w h a t
h a s c t h e d i x
f r o m t x g s a w

Word Box

~~are~~	said
do	saw
from	the
has	went
have	what
must	

WORDS TO KNOW

Words to Know

Student Directions

Follow These Steps

1. Mix up the cards.
   Pile the cards facedown.
   Take 3 cards.

2. Match the cards
   that are the same.

3. Do the activity sheet.

4. Check your answers.

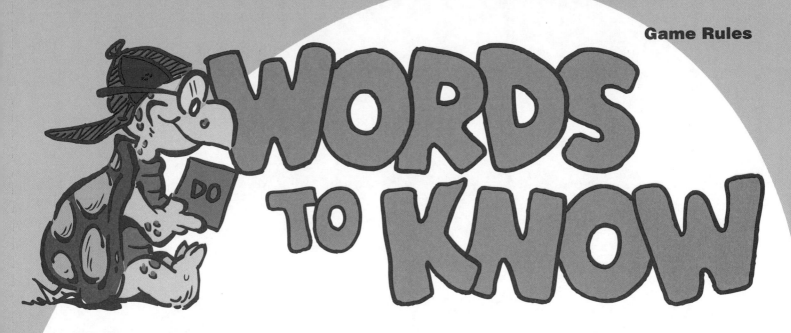

Rules for a Small Group:

1. The object of the game is to make matches.
   Mix up the cards.
   Pile the cards facedown.

2. Take 3 cards.
   Don't show your cards.

3. Take turns. Ask the player next to you for a card.
   If that player has the card, you get it.
   If that player does not have the card,
   you take the top card from the pile.
   Two of the same cards make a match.
   Put the two cards down.

4. Play until all the cards are matched.
   Count your matches.
   The player with the most matches wins.

Rules for 1 Player:

1. Mix up the cards.
   Place the cards facedown in a pile.

2. Take one card at a time.
   See how long it takes to match
   all of the cards.

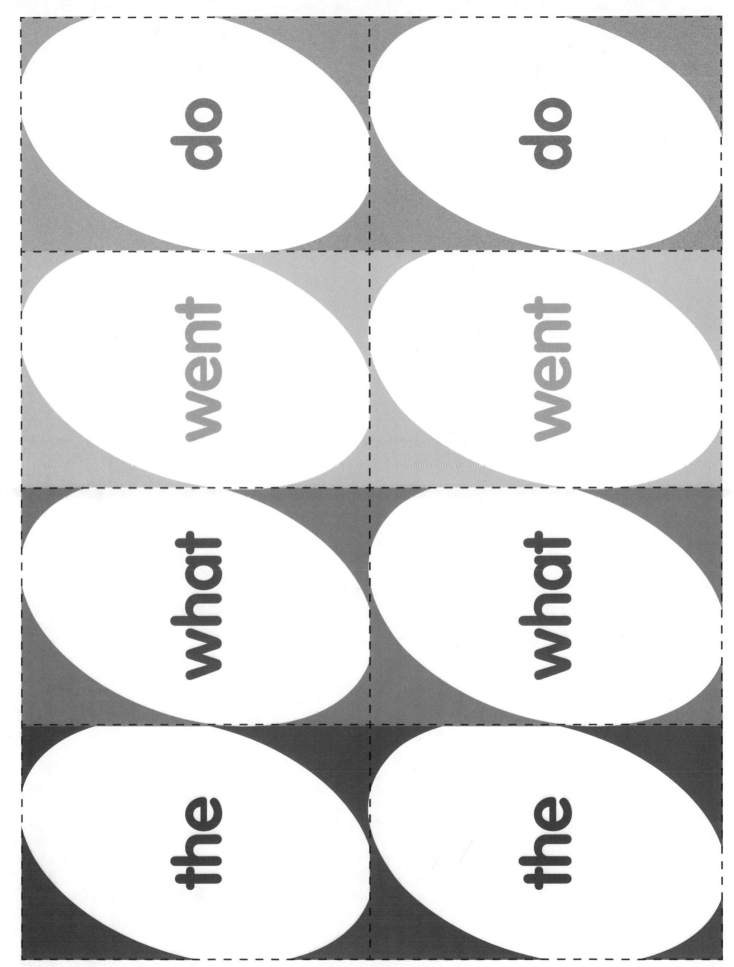

Words to Know

EMC 3347 • © Evan-Moor Corp.

Words to Know

EMC 3347 • © Evan-Moor Corp.

Words to Know

EMC 3347 • © Evan-Moor Corp.

Words to Know

EMC 3347 • © Evan-Moor Corp.

Words to Know

EMC 3347 • © Evan-Moor Corp.

Words to Know

EMC 3347 • © Evan-Moor Corp.

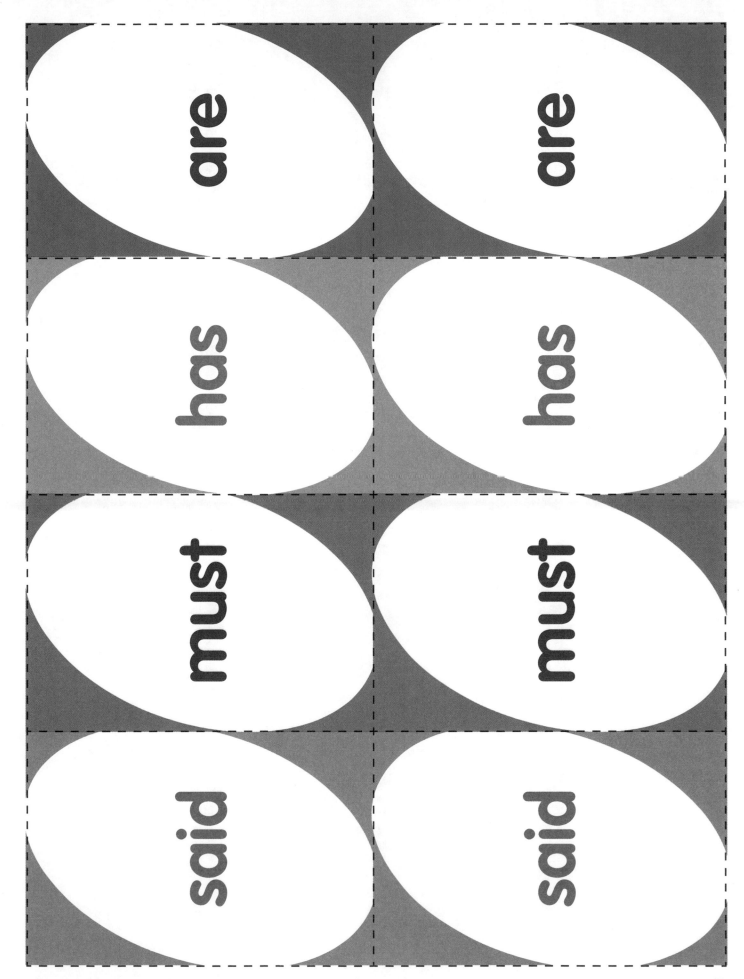

Words to Know
EMC 3347 • © Evan-Moor Corp.

Words to Know
EMC 3347 • © Evan-Moor Corp.

Words to Know
EMC 3347 • © Evan-Moor Corp.

Words to Know
EMC 3347 • © Evan-Moor Corp.

Words to Know
EMC 3347 • © Evan-Moor Corp.

Words to Know
EMC 3347 • © Evan-Moor Corp.

Words to Know
EMC 3347 • © Evan-Moor Corp.

Words to Know
EMC 3347 • © Evan-Moor Corp.

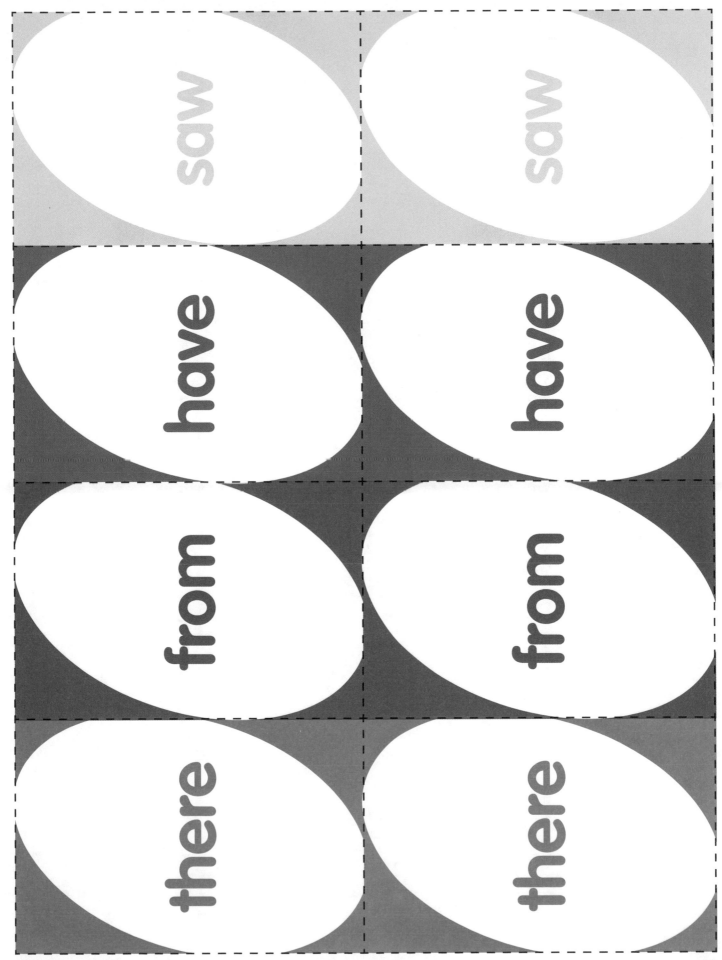

Words to Know
EMC 3347 • © Evan-Moor Corp.

Words to Know
EMC 3347 • © Evan-Moor Corp.

Words to Know
EMC 3347 • © Evan-Moor Corp.

Words to Know
EMC 3347 • © Evan-Moor Corp.

Words to Know
EMC 3347 • © Evan-Moor Corp.

Words to Know
EMC 3347 • © Evan-Moor Corp.

Words to Know

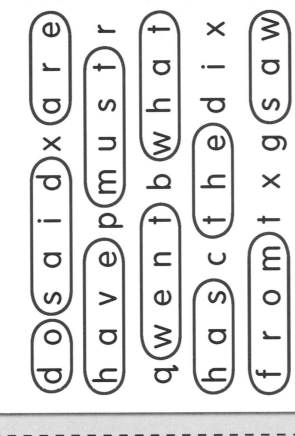

d o	s a i d	x	a r e
h a v e	p	m u s t	r
q	w e n t	b	w h a t
h a s	c	t h e	d i x
f	r o m	t	x g s a w

Lift the flap to check your answers.

Answer Key

In My Suitcase

Preparing the Center

1. Prepare a folder following the directions on page 3.

   Cover—page 57

   Student Directions—page 59

   Sorting Pockets—pages 61 and 63

   Cards—pages 65–71

   Answer Key—page 73

2. Reproduce a supply of the activity sheet on page 56. Place copies in the left-hand pocket of the folder.

Small-Group Practice

1. Place the cards faceup. Have each student select a suitcase. (Some students may need to share.)

2. Next, the students take turns selecting an item that goes into the pocket of the suitcase they chose. The students read their items aloud. The students continue until all the items are packed. The cards are self-checking.

3. Then the students work cooperatively to complete their own activity sheet.

4. Finally, the students check their answers using the answer key.

Independent Practice

1. The student places the cards faceup.

2. Next, the student selects one suitcase and packs the six items that go into the pocket of that suitcase. The student reads the items aloud. The cards are self-checking. If time allows, the student may pack more than one suitcase.

3. Then the student completes the activity sheet.

4. Finally, the student self-checks by using the answer key.

In My Suitcase

Look at each row.
Color the two things that belong to each person.

Dad	tie	belt	earrings
Mom	bib	dress	purse
Timmy	boots	rattle	T-shirt
Baby	wallet	booties	diaper

IN MY SUITCASE

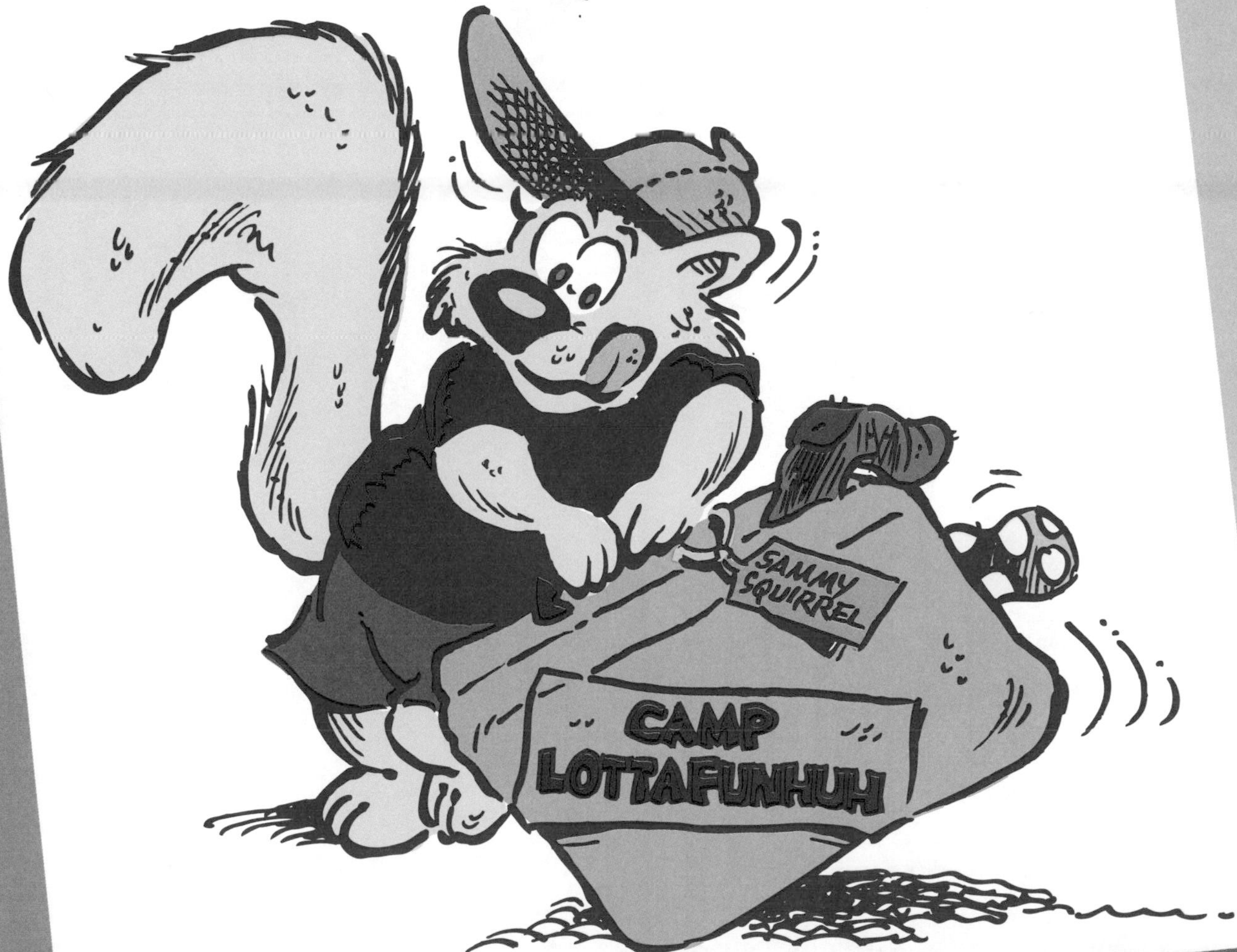

In My Suitcase

Follow These Steps

1. Take the suitcases.

2. Put the cards inside the correct suitcases.

3. Turn the cards over to check your work.

4. Do the activity sheet.

5. Check the answers.

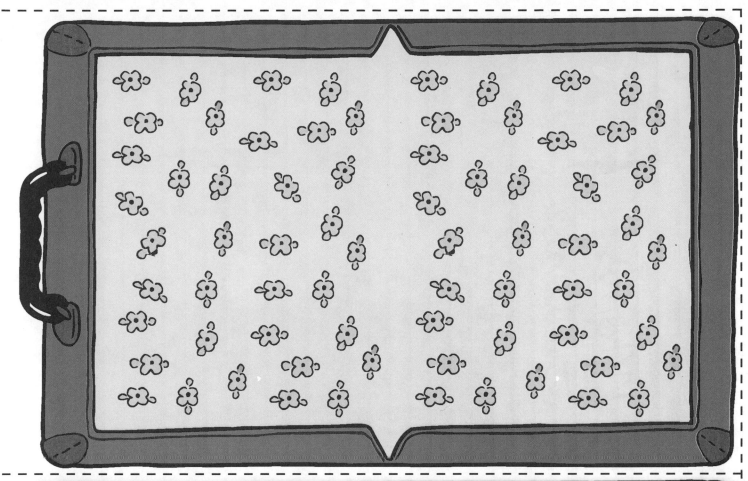

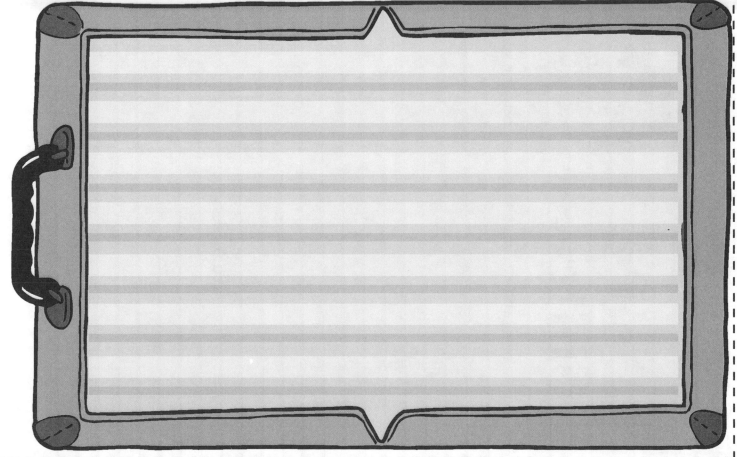

fold

fold

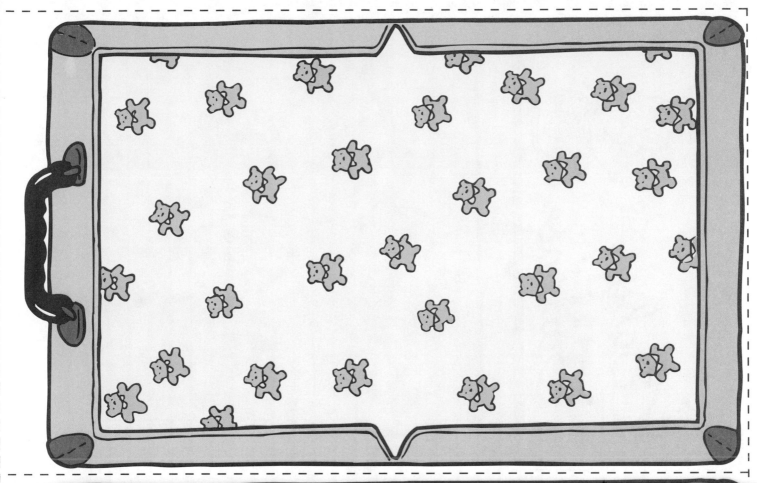

Baby's Suitcase

Timmy's Suitcase

In My Suitcase
EMC 3347 • © Evan-Moor Corp.

fold

In My Suitcase
EMC 3347 • © Evan-Moor Corp.

fold

tie

socks

pants

wallet

belt

coat

Dad

In My Suitcase
EMC 3347 • © Evan-Moor Corp.

Dad

In My Suitcase
EMC 3347 • © Evan-Moor Corp.

Dad

In My Suitcase
EMC 3347 • © Evan-Moor Corp.

Dad

In My Suitcase
EMC 3347 • © Evan-Moor Corp.

Dad

In My Suitcase
EMC 3347 • © Evan-Moor Corp.

Dad

In My Suitcase
EMC 3347 • © Evan-Moor Corp.

blouse

skirt

shoes

dress

purse

earrings

Mom

In My Suitcase
EMC 3347 • © Evan-Moor Corp.

Mom

In My Suitcase
EMC 3347 • © Evan-Moor Corp.

Mom

In My Suitcase
EMC 3347 • © Evan-Moor Corp.

Mom

In My Suitcase
EMC 3347 • © Evan-Moor Corp.

Mom

In My Suitcase
EMC 3347 • © Evan-Moor Corp.

Mom

In My Suitcase
EMC 3347 • © Evan-Moor Corp.

jeans

T-shirt

boots

cap

pajamas

bathrobe

Timmy

In My Suitcase
EMC 3347 • © Evan-Moor Corp.

Timmy

In My Suitcase
EMC 3347 • © Evan-Moor Corp.

Timmy

In My Suitcase
EMC 3347 • © Evan-Moor Corp.

Timmy

In My Suitcase
EMC 3347 • © Evan-Moor Corp.

Timmy

In My Suitcase
EMC 3347 • © Evan-Moor Corp.

Timmy

In My Suitcase
EMC 3347 • © Evan-Moor Corp.

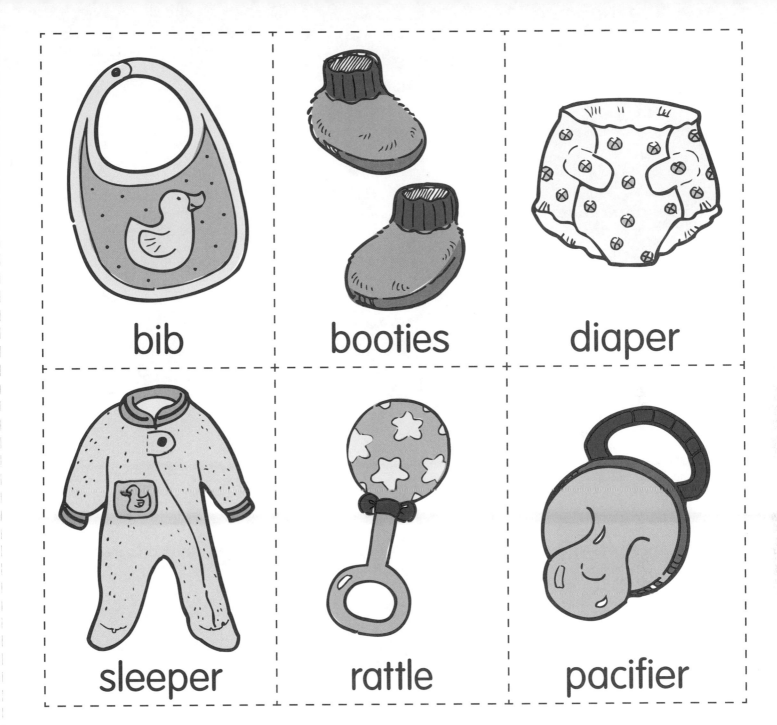

bib

booties

diaper

sleeper

rattle

pacifier

Baby

In My Suitcase
EMC 3347 • © Evan-Moor Corp.

Baby

In My Suitcase
EMC 3347 • © Evan-Moor Corp.

Baby

In My Suitcase
EMC 3347 • © Evan-Moor Corp.

Baby

In My Suitcase
EMC 3347 • © Evan-Moor Corp.

Baby

In My Suitcase
EMC 3347 • © Evan-Moor Corp.

Baby

In My Suitcase
EMC 3347 • © Evan-Moor Corp.

In My Suitcase

earrings	belt	tie	Dad
purse	dress	bib	Mom
T-shirt	rattle	boots	Timmy
diaper	booties	wallet	Baby

IN MY SUITCASE

Lift the flap to check your answers.

School Fun

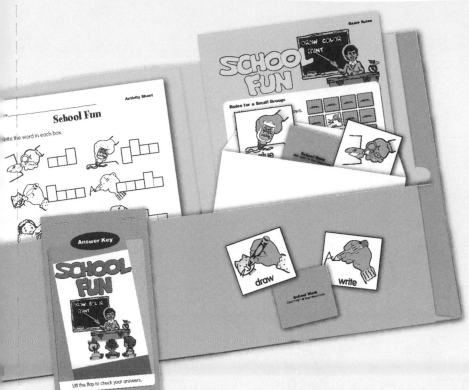

Preparing the Center

1. Prepare a folder following the directions on page 3.

    Cover—page 77

    Student Directions—page 79

    Game Rules—page 81

    Cards—pages 83 and 85

    Answer Key—page 87

2. Reproduce a supply of the activity sheet on page 76. Place copies in the left-hand pocket of the folder.

Small-Group Practice	Independent Practice
1. Review the game rules with the students. Arrange the cards as shown in the rules. Have the students practice reading the school action words before beginning the game.	1. Review the game rules with the student. Arrange the cards as shown in the rules. Have the student practice reading the school action words before beginning the game.
2. Next, the students play the game. Encourage the students to read the words aloud.	2. Next, the student plays the game, continuing until all matches have been made. Encourage the student to read the words aloud.
3. Then the students work cooperatively to complete their own activity sheet.	3. Then the student completes the activity sheet.
4. Finally, the students check their answers using the answer key.	4. Finally, the student self-checks by using the answer key.

School Fun

Write the word in each box.

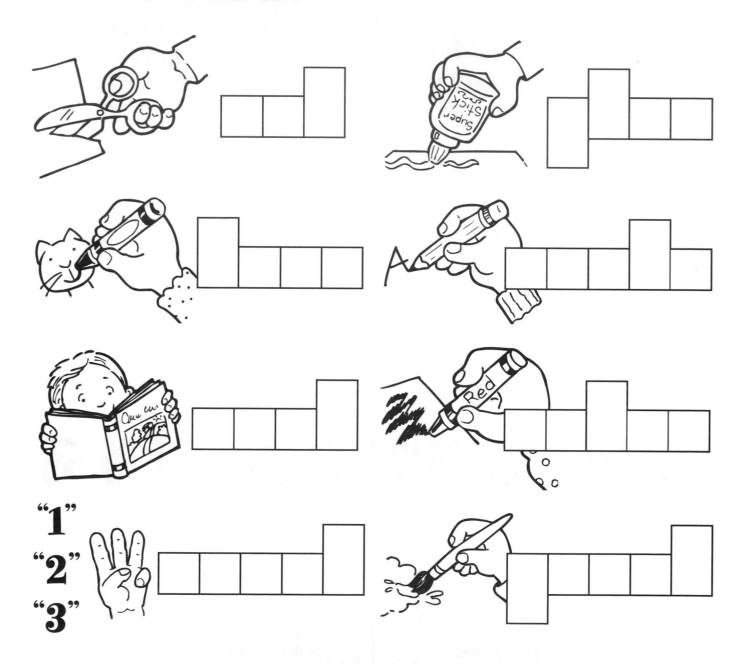

Word Box

color	count	cut	draw
glue	paint	read	write

SCHOOL FUN

DRAW COLOR
PAINT

School Fun

Follow These Steps

1. Place the cards facedown.

2. Play the game.

3. Match all of the cards.

4. Do the activity sheet.

5. Check the answers.

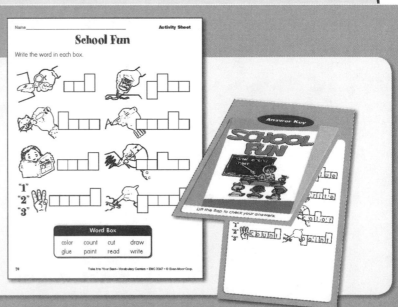

SCHOOL FUN

Rules for a Small Group:

1. Mix up the cards.
   Place them facedown in rows.

2. Take turns.
   Turn two cards over.
   If the cards match, keep them.
   If the cards don't match,
   turn them back over.

3. After the last match,
   count your cards.
   The player with the
   most cards wins.

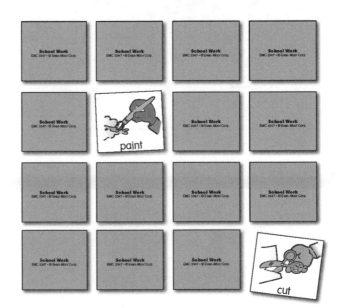

Rules for 1 Player:

1. Mix up the cards.
   Place them facedown in rows.

2. Turn two cards over.
   If the cards match, keep them.
   If the cards don't match,
   turn them back over.

3. Play until you match all
   of the cards.

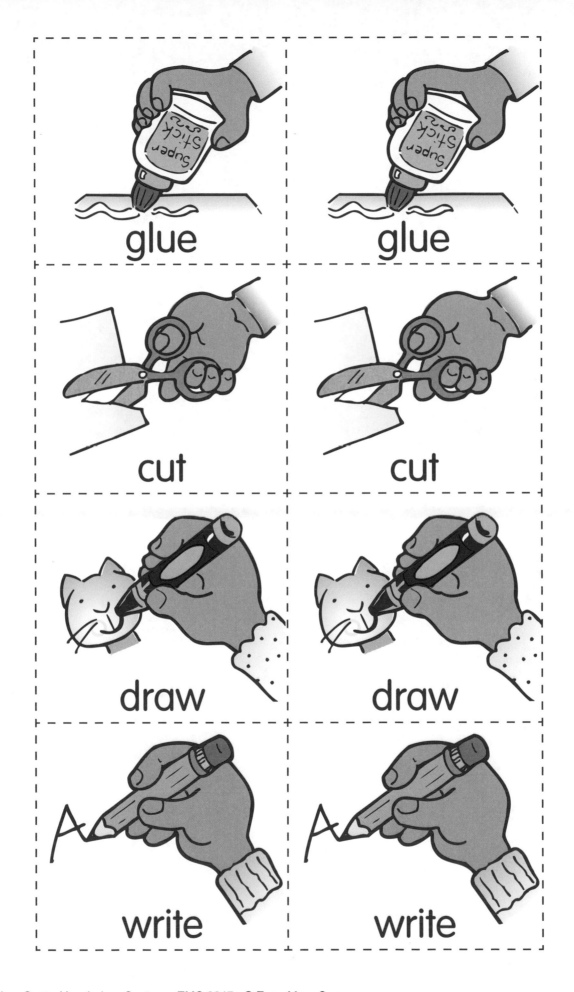

glue

glue

cut

cut

draw

draw

write

write

School Fun
EMC 3347 • © Evan-Moor Corp.

School Fun
EMC 3347 • © Evan-Moor Corp.

School Fun
EMC 3347 • © Evan-Moor Corp.

School Fun
EMC 3347 • © Evan-Moor Corp.

School Fun
EMC 3347 • © Evan-Moor Corp.

School Fun
EMC 3347 • © Evan-Moor Corp.

School Fun
EMC 3347 • © Evan-Moor Corp.

School Fun
EMC 3347 • © Evan-Moor Corp.

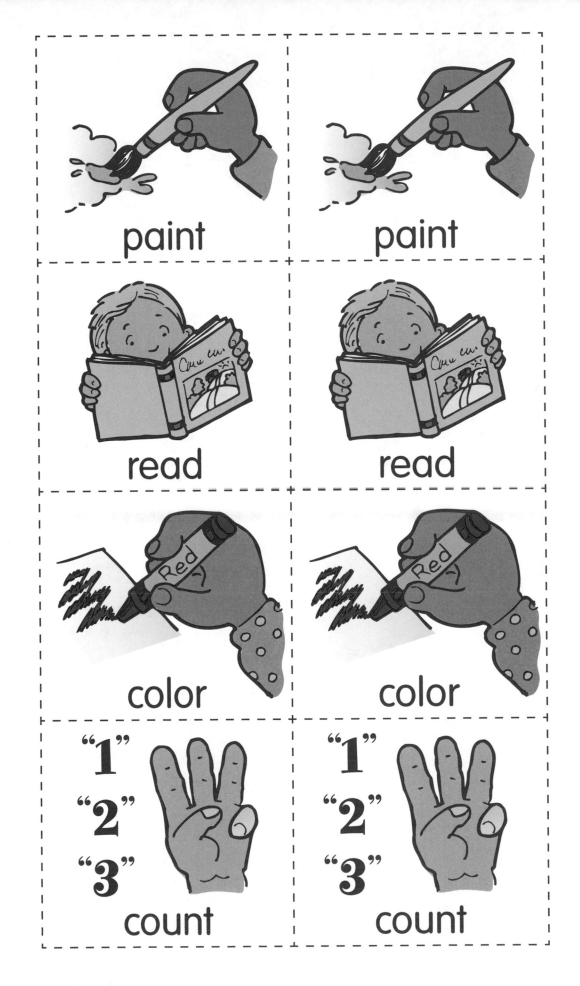

paint paint

read read

color color

"1"
"2"
"3"
count

"1"
"2"
"3"
count

School Fun
EMC 3347 • © Evan-Moor Corp.

School Fun
EMC 3347 • © Evan-Moor Corp.

School Fun
EMC 3347 • © Evan-Moor Corp.

School Fun
EMC 3347 • © Evan-Moor Corp.

School Fun
EMC 3347 • © Evan-Moor Corp.

School Fun
EMC 3347 • © Evan-Moor Corp.

School Fun
EMC 3347 • © Evan-Moor Corp.

School Fun
EMC 3347 • © Evan-Moor Corp.

School Fun

g l u e	c u t		
w r i t e	d r a w		
c o l o r	r e a d		
p a i n t	c o u n t	"1" "2" "3"	

Lift the flap to check your answers.

Make a Word

Preparing the Center

1. Prepare a folder following the directions on page 3.

    Cover—page 91

    Student Directions—page 93

    Puzzle Pieces—pages 95–99

    Answer Key—page 101

2. Reproduce a supply of the activity sheet on page 90. Place copies in the left-hand pocket of the folder.

Small-Group Practice	Independent Practice
1. The students place all of the puzzle pieces faceup. Give each student the initial letter of one of the word puzzles.	1. The student places all of the puzzle pieces faceup. Give the student the initial letter of one of the word puzzles.
2. Next, the students complete their word puzzle by connecting two pieces. They take turns reading their word aloud.	2. Next, the student completes the word puzzle by connecting two pieces. The student reads the word aloud.
3. The students complete all of the word puzzles, using the pictures as guides.	3. The student completes all of the word puzzles, using the pictures as guides.
4. Then the students work cooperatively to complete their own activity sheet.	4. Then the student completes the activity sheet.
5. Finally, the students check their answers using the answer key.	5. Finally, the student self-checks by using the answer key.

Make a Word

Say the name of the picture.
Use the letters to write the word.

n p e	m j a	a g b

_ _ _	_ _ _	_ _ _
b t u	e v t	a p m
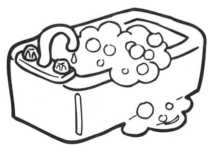		
_ _ _	_ _ _	_ _ _
o g l	a v n	e n t

_ _ _	_ _ _	_ _ _

Make a Word

Follow These Steps

1. Spread out the puzzle pieces.

2. Make words.

3. Do the activity sheet.

4. Check the answers.

pen

Make a Word

EMC 3347 • © Evan-Moor Corp.

pen

Make a Word

EMC 3347 • © Evan-Moor Corp.

pen

Make a Word

EMC 3347 • © Evan-Moor Corp.

tub

Make a Word

EMC 3347 • © Evan-Moor Corp.

tub

Make a Word

EMC 3347 • © Evan-Moor Corp.

tub

Make a Word

EMC 3347 • © Evan-Moor Corp.

vet

Make a Word

EMC 3347 • © Evan-Moor Corp.

vet

Make a Word

EMC 3347 • © Evan-Moor Corp.

vet

Make a Word

EMC 3347 • © Evan-Moor Corp.

m a p

j a m

v a n

map

Make a Word

EMC 3347 • © Evan-Moor Corp.

map

Make a Word

EMC 3347 • © Evan-Moor Corp.

map

Make a Word

EMC 3347 • © Evan-Moor Corp.

jam

Make a Word

EMC 3347 • © Evan-Moor Corp.

jam

Make a Word

EMC 3347 • © Evan-Moor Corp.

jam

Make a Word

EMC 3347 • © Evan-Moor Corp.

van

Make a Word

EMC 3347 • © Evan-Moor Corp.

van

Make a Word

EMC 3347 • © Evan-Moor Corp.

van

Make a Word

EMC 3347 • © Evan-Moor Corp.

log

Make a Word
EMC 3347 • © Evan-Moor Corp.

log

Make a Word
EMC 3347 • © Evan-Moor Corp.

log

Make a Word
EMC 3347 • © Evan-Moor Corp.

net

Make a Word
EMC 3347 • © Evan-Moor Corp.

net

Make a Word
EMC 3347 • © Evan-Moor Corp.

net

Make a Word
EMC 3347 • © Evan-Moor Corp.

bag

Make a Word
EMC 3347 • © Evan-Moor Corp.

bag

Make a Word
EMC 3347 • © Evan-Moor Corp.

bag

Make a Word
EMC 3347 • © Evan-Moor Corp.

Make a Word

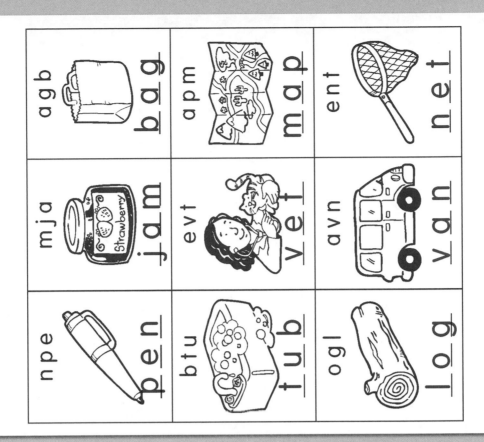

a g b **b a g**	m j a **j a m**	n p e **p e n**
a p m **m a p**	e v t **v e t**	b t u **t u b**
e n t **n e t**	a v n **v a n**	o g l **l o g**

Lift the flap to check your answers.

Two Words in One

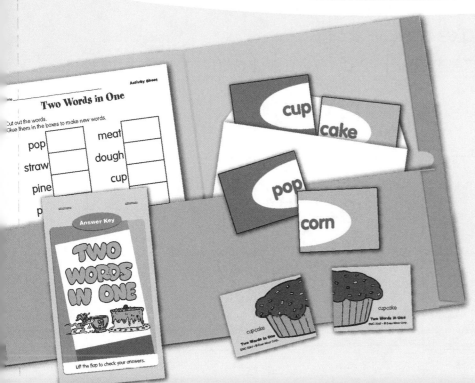

Preparing the Center

1. Prepare a folder following the directions on page 3.

   Cover—page 105

   Student Directions—page 107

   Word Cards—pages 109–113

   Answer Key—page 115

2. Reproduce a supply of the activity sheet on page 104. Place copies in the left-hand pocket of the folder.

Small-Group Practice

1. The students scatter the word cards, word side up. The students each take one purple word card.

2. Next, one student at a time finds the green card that goes with the purple card to make a compound word. Encourage the students to read the compound words aloud. The students turn over the cards to check their work.

3. Then the students work cooperatively to complete their own activity sheet.

4. Finally, the students check their answers using the answer key.

Independent Practice

1. The student scatters the word cards, word side up.

2. Next, the student matches a purple card with a green card to make a compound word. Encourage the student to read the compound word aloud. The student turns over the cards to check his or her work.

3. Then the student completes the activity sheet.

4. Finally, the student self-checks by using the answer key.

Two Words in One

Cut out the words.
Glue them in the boxes to make new words.

pop	
straw	
pine	
pea	
water	

meat	
dough	
cup	
pan	

apple

| ball | berry | cake | cake |
| corn | melon | nut | nut |

TWO WORDS IN ONE

cupcake

Two Words in One
EMC 3347 • © Evan-Moor Corp.

cupcake

Two Words in One
EMC 3347 • © Evan-Moor Corp.

Follow These Steps

1. Place the words faceup.

2. Read the words.
   Put a purple card and
   a green card together
   to make a new word.
   Turn the cards over
   to check your work.

3. Do the activity sheet.

4. Check the answers.

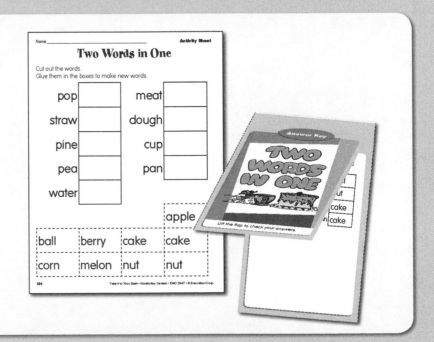

pop|corn

cup|cake

pea|nut

popcorn

Two Words in One

popcorn

Two Words in One

cupcake

Two Words in One

cupcake

Two Words in One

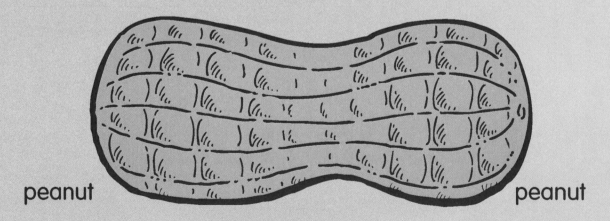

peanut

Two Words in One

peanut

Two Words in One

straw berry

water melon

meat ball

strawberry

Two Words in One

EMC 3347 • © Evan-Moor Corp.

strawberry

Two Words in One

EMC 3347 • © Evan-Moor Corp.

watermelon

Two Words in One

EMC 3347 • © Evan-Moor Corp.

watermelon

Two Words in One

EMC 3347 • © Evan-Moor Corp.

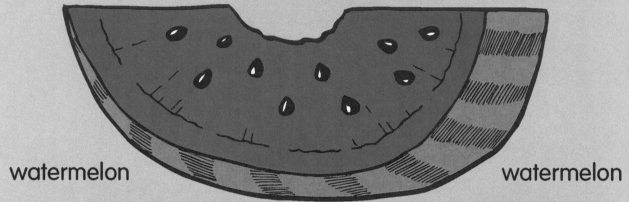

meatball

Two Words in One

EMC 3347 • © Evan-Moor Corp.

meatball

Two Words in One

EMC 3347 • © Evan-Moor Corp.

pine apple

pan cake

dough nut

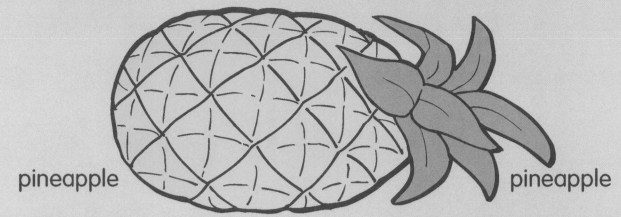

pineapple

pineapple

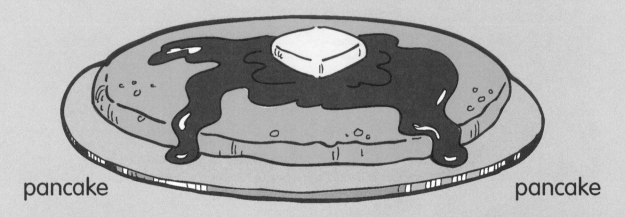

pancake

pancake

doughnut

doughnut

Two Words in One

pop	corn
straw	berry
pine	apple
pea	nut
water	melon

meat	ball
dough	nut
cup	cake
pan	cake

Lift the flap to check your answers.

"Ow" Words

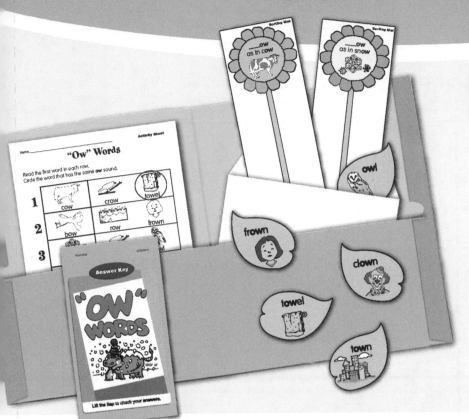

Preparing the Center

1. Prepare a folder following the directions on page 3.

   Cover—page 119

   Student Directions—page 121

   Mats, Leaves—pages 123–127

   Answer Key—page 129

2. Reproduce a supply of the activity sheet on page 118. Place copies in the left-hand pocket of the folder.

Small-Group Practice

1. Place the two flower mats on a flat surface and scatter the leaves faceup. Model the steps in completing the word families. Read the *ow* sound on each flower. Choose a leaf, read its word aloud, and place the leaf on the flower with the same *ow* sound.

2. Next, have each student do as you had modeled. Have the students continue until they place all the leaves. The students turn over the leaves to check their work.

3. Then the students work cooperatively to complete their own activity sheet.

4. Finally, the students check their answers using the answer key.

Independent Practice

1. Place the two flower mats on a flat surface and scatter the leaves faceup. Model the steps in completing the word families. Read the *ow* sound on each flower. Choose a leaf, read its word aloud, and place the leaf on the flower with the same *ow* sound.

2. Next, the student does as you had modeled. The student continues until all leaves are placed, and then turns the leaves over to check his or her work.

3. Then the student completes the activity sheet.

4. Finally, the student self-checks by using the answer key.

"Ow" Words

Read the first word in each row.
Circle the word that has the same **ow** sound.

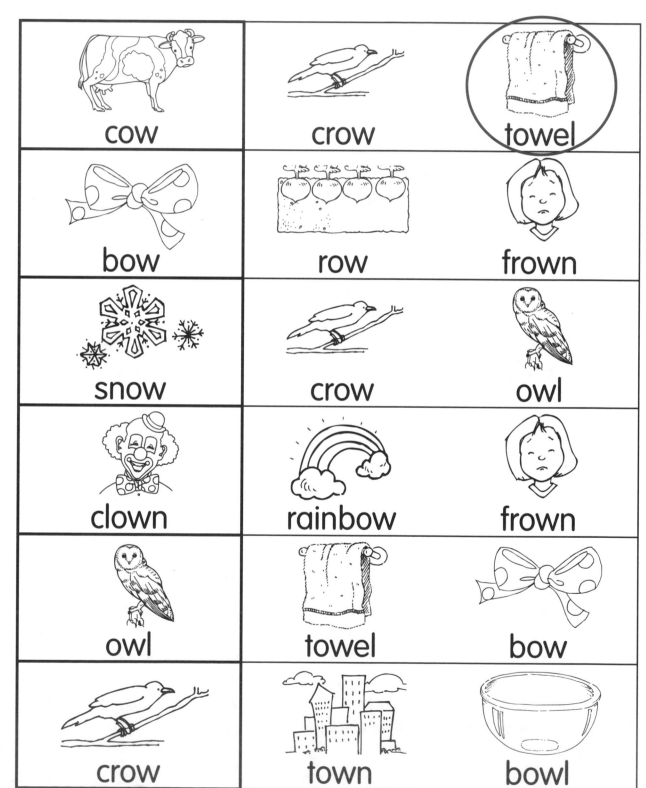

1 cow	crow	(towel)
2 bow	row	frown
3 snow	crow	owl
4 clown	rainbow	frown
5 owl	towel	bow
6 crow	town	bowl

Take It to Your Seat—Vocabulary Centers • EMC 3347 • © Evan-Moor Corp.

"Ow" Words
Student Directions

Follow These Steps

1. Take the two flowers.

2. Read the words. Place each leaf on the flower with the same **ow** sound. Turn the leaves over to check your work.

3. Do the activity sheet.

4. Check the answers.

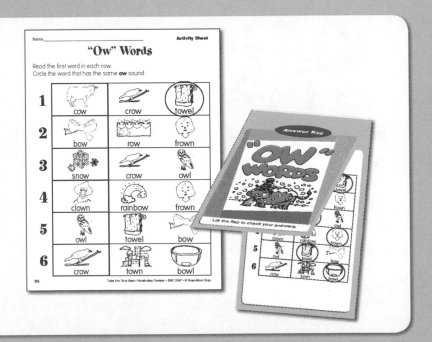

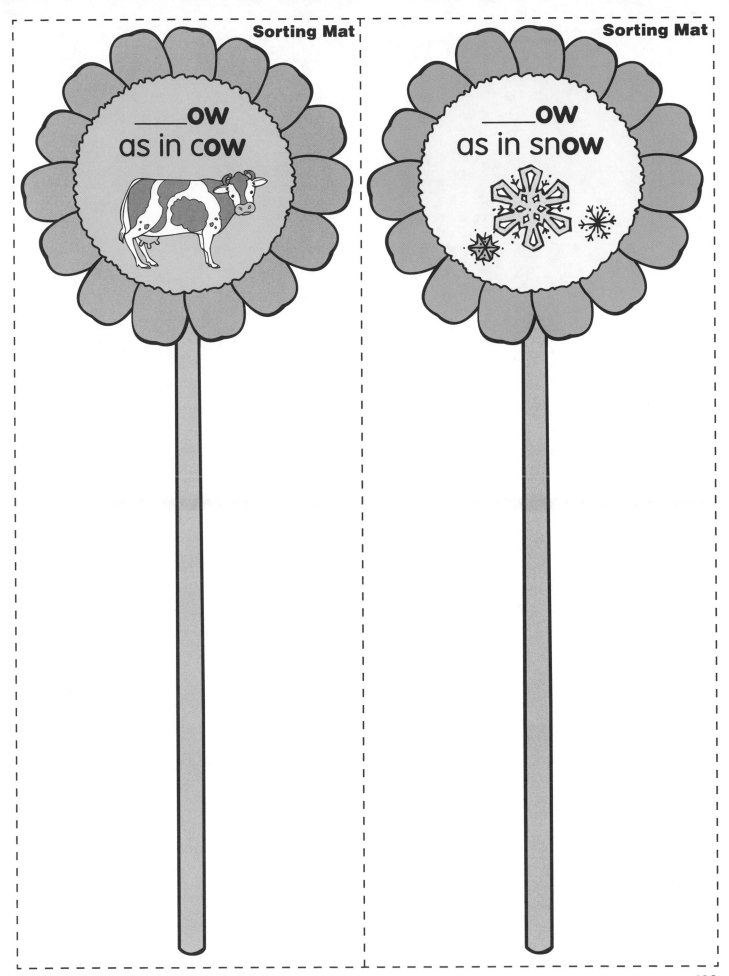

___ow
as in c**ow**

___ow
as in sn**ow**

"Ow" Words

EMC 3347 • © Evan-Moor Corp.

"Ow" Words

EMC 3347 • © Evan-Moor Corp.

frown

owl

towel

clown

town

"Ow" Words

EMC 3347 • © Evan-Moor Corp.

"Ow" Words

EMC 3347 • © Evan-Moor Corp.

"Ow" Words

EMC 3347 • © Evan-Moor Corp.

"Ow" Words

EMC 3347 • © Evan-Moor Corp.

"Ow" Words

EMC 3347 • © Evan-Moor Corp.

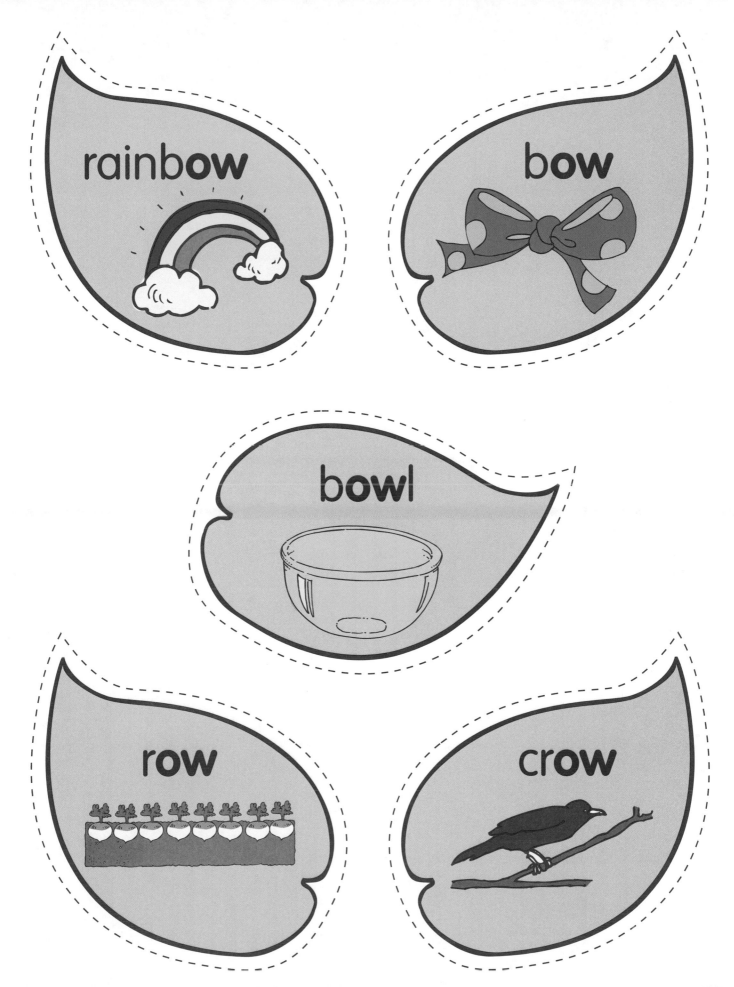

rainbow

bow

bowl

row

crow

"Ow" Words

EMC 3347 • © Evan-Moor Corp.

"Ow" Words

EMC 3347 • © Evan-Moor Corp.

"Ow" Words

EMC 3347 • © Evan-Moor Corp.

"Ow" Words

EMC 3347 • © Evan-Moor Corp.

"Ow" Words

EMC 3347 • © Evan-Moor Corp.

"Ow" Words

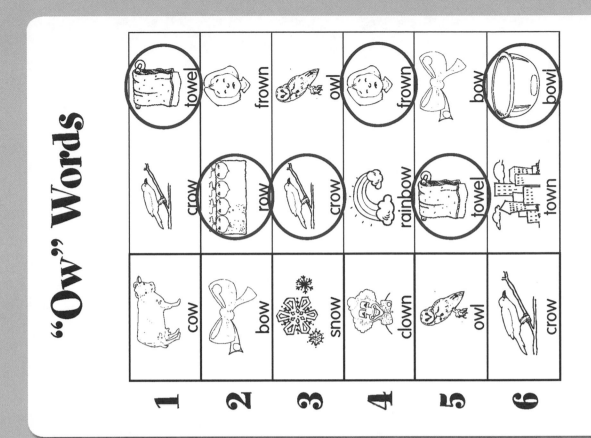

1	cow	crow	towel
2	bow	row	frown
3	snow	crow	owl
4	clown	rainbow	frown
5	owl	towel	bow
6	crow	town	bowl

Lift the flap to check your answers.

Opposites

Preparing the Center

1. Prepare a folder following the directions on page 3.

   > Cover—page 133
   >
   > Student Directions—page 135
   >
   > Puzzle Pieces—pages 137–141
   >
   > Answer Key—page 143

2. Reproduce a supply of the activity sheet on page 132. Place copies in the left-hand pocket of the folder.

Small-Group Practice

1. The students separate the puzzle pieces by color and spread them out faceup.

2. Next, the students take turns putting together blue pieces and yellow pieces to match words with opposite meanings. Have the students read their opposites aloud.

3. Then the students work cooperatively to complete their own activity sheet.

4. Finally, the students check their answers using the answer key.

Independent Practice

1. The student separates the puzzle pieces by color and spreads them out faceup.

2. Next, the student puts together blue pieces and yellow pieces to match words with opposite meanings. Encourage the student to read the opposites aloud.

3. Then the student completes the activity sheet.

4. Finally, the student self-checks by using the answer key.

Opposites

Write the opposite.
Write the letters in the boxes.

1.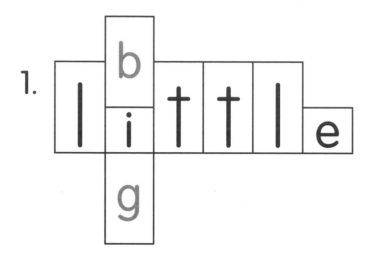
l i t t l e
with b i g vertical

2.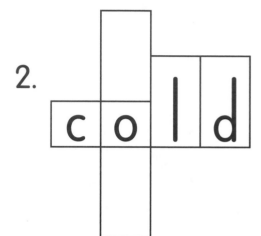
c o l d

3.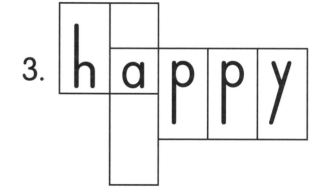
h a p p y

4.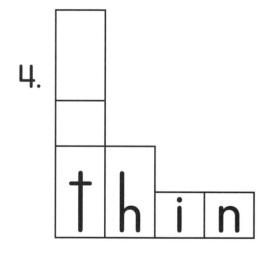
t h i n

5.
s l o w

6. y o u n g

OPPOSITES

Opposites

Follow These Steps

1. Spread out the puzzle pieces.

2. Match the opposites.

3. Do the activity sheet.

4. Check the answers.

Name _____   Activity Sheet

Opposites

Write the opposite.
Write the letters in the boxes.

1. little (with b, i, g vertical)
2. cold
3. happy
4. thin
5. slow
6. young

Take It to Your Seat—Vocabulary Centers • EMC 3347 • © Evan-Moor Corp.

cold

hot

plain

fancy

big

little

old

young

Opposites

EMC 3347 • © Evan-Moor Corp.

Opposites

EMC 3347 • © Evan-Moor Corp.

Opposites

EMC 3347 • © Evan-Moor Corp.

Opposites

EMC 3347 • © Evan-Moor Corp.

Opposites

EMC 3347 • © Evan-Moor Corp.

Opposites

EMC 3347 • © Evan-Moor Corp.

Opposites

EMC 3347 • © Evan-Moor Corp.

Opposites

EMC 3347 • © Evan-Moor Corp.

happy

sad

tall

short

sour

sweet

wide

narrow

Opposites
EMC 3347 • © Evan-Moor Corp.

Opposites
EMC 3347 • © Evan-Moor Corp.

Opposites
EMC 3347 • © Evan-Moor Corp.

Opposites
EMC 3347 • © Evan-Moor Corp.

Opposites
EMC 3347 • © Evan-Moor Corp.

Opposites
EMC 3347 • © Evan-Moor Corp.

Opposites
EMC 3347 • © Evan-Moor Corp.

Opposites
EMC 3347 • © Evan-Moor Corp.

hard

soft

wet

dry

fast

slow

fat

thin

Opposites

EMC 3347 • © Evan-Moor Corp.

Opposites

EMC 3347 • © Evan-Moor Corp.

Opposites

EMC 3347 • © Evan-Moor Corp.

Opposites

EMC 3347 • © Evan-Moor Corp.

Opposites

EMC 3347 • © Evan-Moor Corp.

Opposites

EMC 3347 • © Evan-Moor Corp.

Opposites

EMC 3347 • © Evan-Moor Corp.

Opposites

EMC 3347 • © Evan-Moor Corp.

Opposites

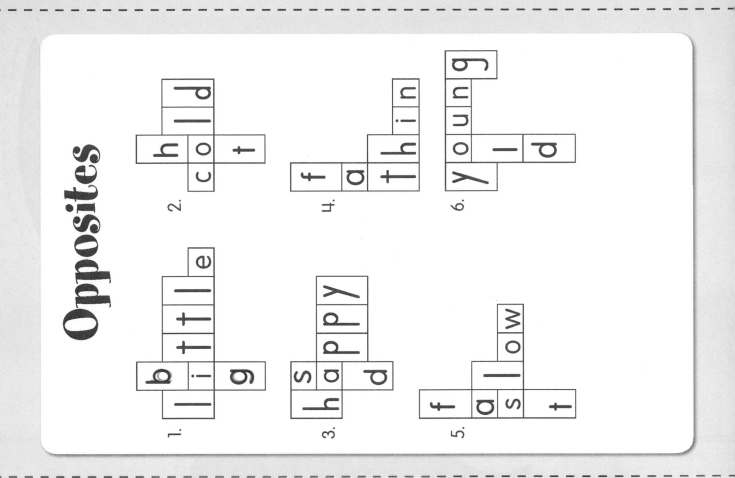

1. l i t t l e / b i g
2. h o l d / c o l d / t (hot / cold)
3. h a p p y / s a d
4. f a t / t h i n
5. f a s t / s l o w
6. y o u n g / o l d

Answer Key

OPPOSITES

Lift the flap to check your answers.

First in Line

Preparing the Center

1. Prepare a folder following the directions on page 3.

   Cover—page 147

   Student Directions—page 149

   Sorting Mats—pages 151–155

   Word Cards—page 157

   Answer Key—page 159

2. Reproduce a supply of the activity sheet on page 146. Place copies in the left-hand pocket of the folder.

Small-Group Practice

1. The students place the mats and word cards faceup, with the mats in the same order as in the book.

2. The students take turns reading each word card aloud. The group decides where the number belongs on the mats. Encourage the group to describe the location using the ordinal number: "The dog is first." The cards are self-checking.

3. Then the students work cooperatively to complete their own activity sheet. They may use the word cards for help in spelling.

4. Finally, the students check their answers using the answer key.

Independent Practice

1. The student places the mats and word cards faceup, with the mats in the same order as in the book.

2. The student reads each word card and places it in the correct location on the mats. The student describes the location aloud using the ordinal number: "The dog is first." The cards are self-checking.

3. Then the student completes the activity sheet. The student may refer to the word cards for help in spelling.

4. Finally, the student self-checks by using the answer key.

First in Line

Look at the animals.
Write the answers.

1. In which place is the  ? _____

2. In which place is the  ? _____

3. In which place is the _____

4. Which animal is between
first and third place? _____

FIRST IN LINE

First in Line

first

third

First in Line
EMC 3347 • © Evan-Moor Corp.

fifth

seventh

First in Line
EMC 3347 • © Evan-Moor Corp.

Follow These Steps

1. Take the sorting mats and word cards.

2. Read the words.
   Place the cards on the mats.
   Turn the cards over to check your work.

3. Do the activity sheet.

4. Check the answers.

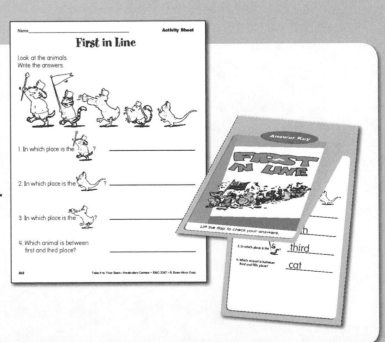

first	second
third	fourth
fifth	sixth
seventh	eighth
ninth	tenth

First in Line

EMC 3347 • © Evan-Moor Corp.

First in Line

EMC 3347 • © Evan-Moor Corp.

First in Line

EMC 3347 • © Evan-Moor Corp.

First in Line

EMC 3347 • © Evan-Moor Corp.

First in Line

EMC 3347 • © Evan-Moor Corp.

First in Line

EMC 3347 • © Evan-Moor Corp.

First in Line

EMC 3347 • © Evan-Moor Corp.

First in Line

EMC 3347 • © Evan-Moor Corp.

First in Line

EMC 3347 • © Evan-Moor Corp.

First in Line

EMC 3347 • © Evan-Moor Corp.

First in Line

first

fifth

third

cat

1. In which place is the [dog]?

2. In which place is the [cat]?

3. In which place is the [horse]?

4. Which animal is between first and third place?

Lift the flap to check your answers.

Animal Babies

Preparing the Center

1. Prepare a folder following the directions on page 3.

   Cover—page 163

   Student Directions—page 165

   Puzzle Pieces—pages 167–173

   Answer Key—page 175

2. Reproduce a supply of the activity sheet on page 162. Place copies in the left-hand pocket of the folder.

Small-Group Practice

1. The students place all puzzle pieces faceup. Each student takes a puzzle piece of an animal mother.

2. Next, the students match the correct animal baby with its mother.

3. The students take turns until they complete all of the puzzles. Help the students read the names of the animals.

4. Then the students work cooperatively to complete their own activity sheet.

5. Finally, the students check their answers using the answer key.

Independent Practice

1. The student places all puzzle pieces faceup.

2. Next, the student completes all of the puzzles by matching the correct animal mother with its baby. Help the student read the names of the animals.

3. Then the student completes the activity sheet.

4. Finally, the student self-checks by using the answer key.

Animal Babies

Color each baby and its mother.
Make them look the same.

1. kitten

2. piglet

3. bunny

4. kid

5. calf

6. pinkie

ANIMAL BABIES

Animal Babies

Student Directions

Follow These Steps

1. Spread out the puzzle pieces.

2. Match the mothers with their babies.

3. Do the activity sheet.

4. Check the answers.

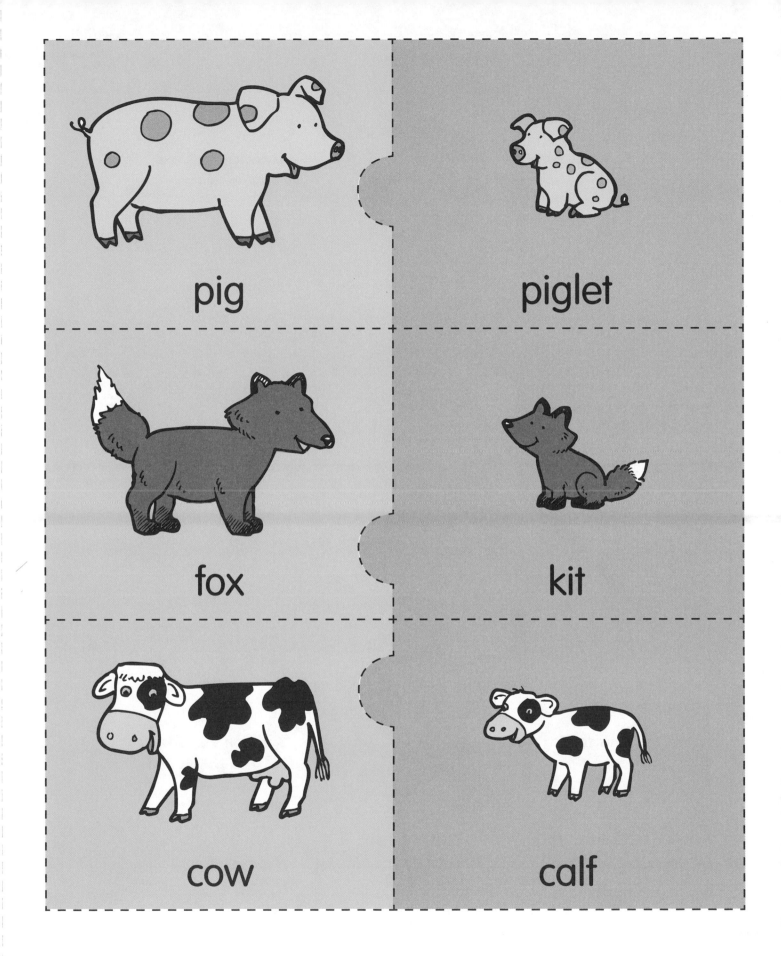

pig

piglet

fox

kit

cow

calf

Animal Babies

EMC 3347 • © Evan-Moor Corp.

Animal Babies

EMC 3347 • © Evan-Moor Corp.

Animal Babies

EMC 3347 • © Evan-Moor Corp.

Animal Babies

EMC 3347 • © Evan-Moor Corp.

Animal Babies

EMC 3347 • © Evan-Moor Corp.

Animal Babies

EMC 3347 • © Evan-Moor Corp.

lion

cub

goat

kid

deer

fawn

Animal Babies

EMC 3347 • © Evan-Moor Corp.

Animal Babies

EMC 3347 • © Evan-Moor Corp.

Animal Babies

EMC 3347 • © Evan-Moor Corp.

Animal Babies

EMC 3347 • © Evan-Moor Corp.

Animal Babies

EMC 3347 • © Evan-Moor Corp.

Animal Babies

EMC 3347 • © Evan-Moor Corp.

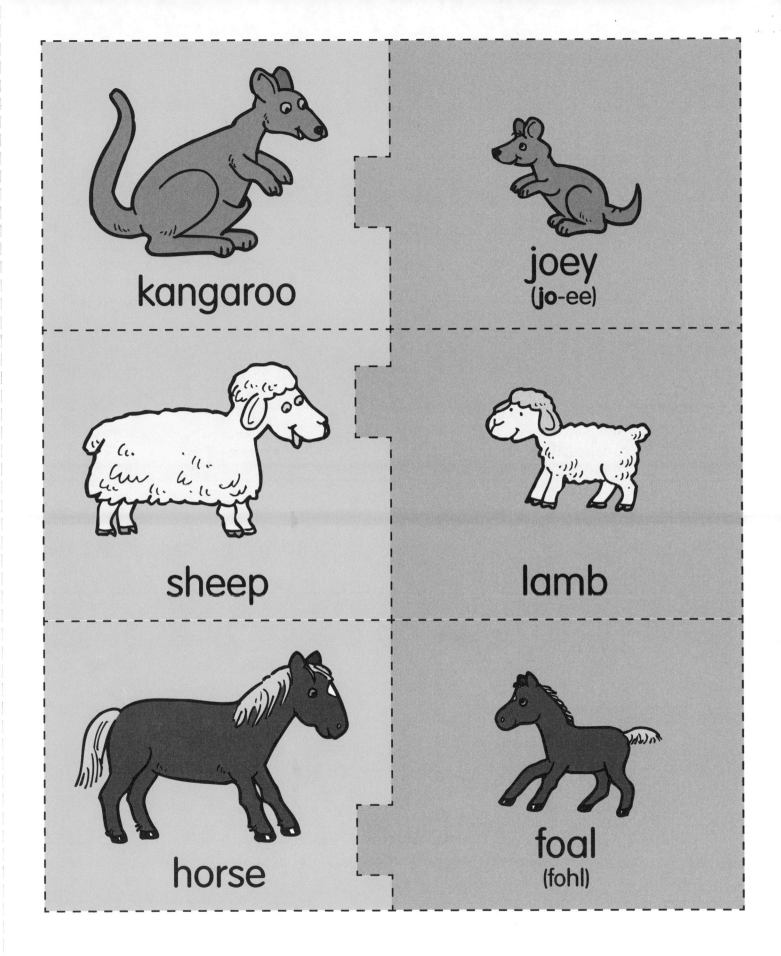

kangaroo

joey
(jo-ee)

sheep

lamb

horse

foal
(fohl)

Animal Babies

EMC 3347 • © Evan-Moor Corp.

Animal Babies

EMC 3347 • © Evan-Moor Corp.

Animal Babies

EMC 3347 • © Evan-Moor Corp.

Animal Babies

EMC 3347 • © Evan-Moor Corp.

Animal Babies

EMC 3347 • © Evan-Moor Corp.

Animal Babies

EMC 3347 • © Evan-Moor Corp.

mouse

pinkie
(**pink**-ee)

rabbit

bunny

cat

kitten

Animal Babies

EMC 3347 • © Evan-Moor Corp.

Animal Babies

EMC 3347 • © Evan-Moor Corp.

Animal Babies

EMC 3347 • © Evan-Moor Corp.

Animal Babies

EMC 3347 • © Evan-Moor Corp.

Animal Babies

EMC 3347 • © Evan-Moor Corp.

Animal Babies

EMC 3347 • © Evan-Moor Corp.

Animal Babies

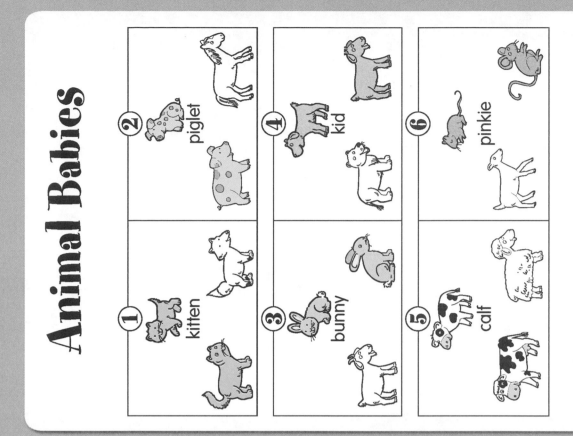

① kitten	② piglet
③ bunny	④ kid
⑤ calf	⑥ pinkie

Lift the flap to check your answers.

Let's Play!

Preparing the Center

1. Prepare a folder following the directions on page 3.

   Cover—page 179

   Student Directions—page 181

   Game Rules—page 183

   Game Boards—pages 185 and 187

   Cards—page 189

   Answer Key—page 191

2. Reproduce a supply of the activity sheet on page 178. Place copies in the left-hand pocket of the folder.

Small-Group Practice

1. Go through the game rules with the students. Provide small objects or paper squares for marking the answers.

2. Next, give students a game board and markers. (Students will need to share boards.) The students take turns playing the game. Encourage the students to read the words aloud as they play.

3. Then the students work cooperatively to complete their own activity sheet.

4. Finally, the students check their answers using the answer key.

Independent Practice

1. Go through the game rules with the student. Provide small objects or paper squares for marking the answers.

2. Next, the student plays the game. Encourage the student to read the words aloud while playing the game.

3. Then the student completes the activity sheet.

4. Finally, the student self-checks by using the answer key.

Let's Play!

Find the words.
Circle the words.

Word Box		
~~bounce~~	jump	roll
run	skate	slide
swim	swing	throw

j u m p x w r u n

t l s w i m u p t

b c f s k a t e z

a (b o u n c e) x o

s w i n g r o l l

z g s l i d e k r

t h r o w z c m o

Let's Play!

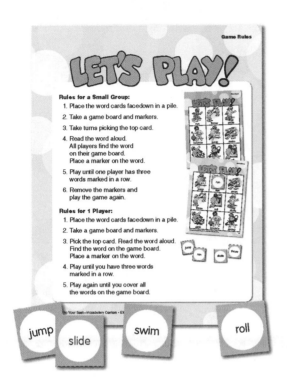

Follow These Steps

1. Take a game board.
   Take the word cards.
   Pile the cards facedown.

2. Play the game.

3. Do the activity sheet.

4. Check the answers.

Rules for a Small Group:

1. Place the word cards facedown in a pile.

2. Take a game board and markers.

3. Take turns picking the top card.

4. Read the word aloud.
   All players find the word
   on their game board.
   Place a marker on the word.

5. Play until one player has three
   words marked in a row.

6. Remove the markers and
   play the game again.

Rules for 1 Player:

1. Place the word cards facedown in a pile.

2. Take a game board and markers.

3. Pick the top card. Read the word aloud.
   Find the word on the game board.
   Place a marker on the word.

4. Play until you have three words
   marked in a row.

5. Play again until you cover all
   the words on the game board.

LET'S PLAY!

run

throw

skate

bounce

jump

swim

slide

swing

roll

LET'S PLAY!

jump

run

swim

throw

roll

skate

slide

bounce

swing

jump	jump	run	run
swim	swim	throw	throw
roll	roll	skate	skate
slide	slide	bounce	bounce
swing	swing		

Let's Play!

EMC 3347

© Evan-Moor Corp.

Let's Play!

EMC 3347

© Evan-Moor Corp.

Let's Play!

EMC 3347

© Evan-Moor Corp.

Let's Play!

EMC 3347

© Evan-Moor Corp.

Let's Play!

EMC 3347

© Evan-Moor Corp.

Let's Play!

EMC 3347

© Evan-Moor Corp.

Let's Play!

EMC 3347

© Evan-Moor Corp.

Let's Play!

EMC 3347

© Evan-Moor Corp.

Let's Play!

EMC 3347

© Evan-Moor Corp.

Let's Play!

EMC 3347

© Evan-Moor Corp.

Let's Play!

EMC 3347

© Evan-Moor Corp.

Let's Play!

EMC 3347

© Evan-Moor Corp.

Let's Play!

EMC 3347

© Evan-Moor Corp.

Let's Play!

EMC 3347

© Evan-Moor Corp.

Let's Play!

EMC 3347

© Evan-Moor Corp.

Let's Play!

EMC 3347

© Evan-Moor Corp.

Let's Play!

EMC 3347

© Evan-Moor Corp.

Let's Play!

EMC 3347

© Evan-Moor Corp.

Let's Play!

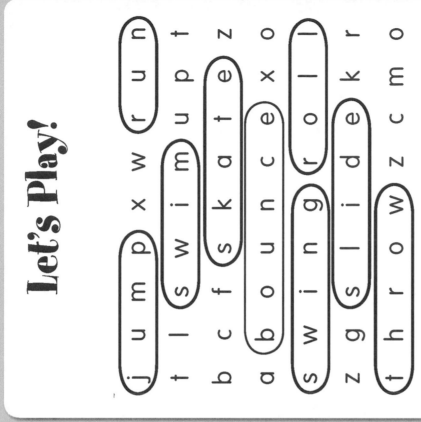

j	u	m	p	x	w	r	u	n
t	l	s	w	i	m	u	p	t
b	c	f	s	k	a	t	e	z
a	b	o	u	n	c	e	x	o
s	w	i	n	g	r	o	l	l
z	g	s	l	i	d	e	k	r
t	h	r	o	w	z	c	m	o

Answer Key

Lift the flap to check your answers.